Keep this pocket-size̶ ̶̶̶̶̶̶̶̶̶̶̶̶̶̶
you are travelling arou̶̶̶̶ ̶̶̶̶̶̶̶̶̶̶̶̶̶̶̶ ̶ ̶̶
holiday.

Whether you are in your car or on foot, you will enjoy an evocative journey back in time. Compare the Nottinghamshire of old with what you can see today—see how the streets have changed, how shops and buildings have been altered or replaced; look at fine details such as lamp-posts, shop fascias and trade signs; and see the many alterations to the Nottinghamshire landscape that have taken place unnoticed during our lives, some of which we may have taken for granted.

At the turn of a page you will gain fascinating insights into Nottinghamshire's unique history.

FRANCIS *FRITH'S*
pocket ALBUM

NOTTINGHAMSHIRE

A POCKET ALBUM

Adapted from an original book by
MARTIN ANDREW

First published in the United Kingdom in 2005 by
Frith Book Company Ltd

ISBN 1-85937-948-6
Text and Design copyright © Frith Book Company Ltd
Photographs copyright © The Francis Frith Collection

British Library Cataloguing in Publication Data

Nottinghamshire—A Pocket Album
Adapted from an original book by Martin Andrew

Frith Book Company Ltd
Frith's Barn, Teffont,
Salisbury, Wiltshire SP3 5QP
Tel: +44 (0) 1722 716 376
 Email: info@francisfrith.co.uk
www.francisfrith.co.uk

Printed and bound in Great Britain by MPG, Bodmin

Front Cover: **NOTTINGHAM**, Wheeler Gate 1902 / 48327T
The colour-tinting is for illustrative purposes only, and is not intended to be historically accurate.

Frontispiece: **NOTTINGHAM**, The Market 1890 / 22808

NOTTINGHAM, Long Row 1890 / 22815

CONTENTS

FRANCIS FRITH
VICTORIAN PIONEER

Francis Frith, founder of the world-famous photographic archive, was a complex and multi-talented man. A devout Quaker and a highly successful Victorian businessman, he was philosophic by nature and pioneering in outlook. By 1855 he had already established a wholesale grocery business in Liverpool, and sold it for the astonishing sum of £200,000, which is the equivalent today of over £15,000,000. Now in his thirties, and captivated by the new science of photography, Frith set out on a series of pioneering journeys up the Nile and to the Near East.

INTRIGUE AND EXPLORATION

He was the first photographer to venture beyond the sixth cataract of the Nile. Africa was still the mysterious 'Dark Continent', and Stanley and Livingstone's historic meeting was a decade into the future. The conditions for picture taking confound belief. He laboured for hours in his wicker dark-room in the sweltering heat of the desert, while the volatile chemicals fizzed dangerously in their trays. Back in London he exhibited his photographs and was 'rapturously cheered' by members of the Royal Society. His reputation as a photographer was made overnight.

VENTURE OF A LIFE-TIME

By the 1870s the railways had threaded their way across the country, and Bank Holidays and half-day Saturdays had been made obligatory by Act of Parliament. All of a sudden the working man and his family were able to enjoy days out, take holidays, and see a little more of the world.

With typical business acumen, Francis Frith foresaw that these new tourists would enjoy having souvenirs to commemorate their days out. For the next thirty years he travelled the country by train and by pony and trap, producing fine photographs of seaside resorts and beauty spots that were keenly bought by millions of Victorians. These prints were painstakingly pasted into family albums and pored over during the dark nights of winter, rekindling precious memories of summer excursions. Frith's studio was soon supplying retail shops all over the country, and by 1890 F Frith & Co had become the greatest specialist photographic publishing company in the world, with over 2,000 sales outlets, and pioneered the picture postcard.

FRANCIS FRITH'S LEGACY

Francis Frith had died in 1898 at his villa in Cannes, his great project still growing. The archive he created continued in business for another seventy years. By 1970 it contained over a third of a million pictures showing 7,000 British towns and villages.

Frith's legacy to us today is of immense significance and value, for the magnificent archive of evocative photographs he created provides a unique record of change in the cities, towns and villages throughout Britain over a century and more. Frith and his fellow studio photographers revisited locations many times down the years to update their views, compiling for us an enthralling and colourful pageant of British life and character.

We are fortunate that Frith was dedicated to recording the minutiae of everyday life. For it is this sheer wealth of visual data, the painstaking chronicle of changes in dress, transport, street layouts, buildings, housing, engineering and landscape that captivates us so much today, offering us a powerful link with the past and with the lives of our ancestors.

Computers have now made it possible for Frith's many thousands of images to be accessed almost instantly. The archive offers every one of us an opportunity to examine the places where we and our families have lived and worked down the years. Its images, depicting our shared past, are now bringing pleasure and enlightenment to millions around the world a century and more after his death.

NOTTINGHAMSHIRE
AN INTRODUCTION

IT IS all the Tourist Board's fault: on any major road entering Nottinghamshire, there is a sign telling you that you are entering Robin Hood Country. While this is an excellent marketing ploy, it does not do justice to this much-underrated county. If Robin Hood existed in the first place, of course his stamping-ground would have been Sherwood Forest, which occupies 100,000 acres of the county's 550,000 acres. Yet if you mention the county to anybody, they will mention Sherwood Forest and the Sheriff of Nottingham. Push a little harder and they might mention D H Lawrence and Trent Bridge cricket ground.

Still, if pursuing the Robin Hood theme brings people to visit and move on to the other delights that Nottinghamshire has to offer, that is all to the good. The official tourist guide lists several Robin Hood attractions: the annual Robin Hood Festival in Sherwood Forest, the annual Robin Hood Pageant at Nottingham Castle, the Tales of Robin Hood experience in Nottingham and the World of Robin Hood near Ollerton - there is even the Robin Hood Way long-distance walk.

Edinstowe is the capital of Robin Hood land, with the Sherwood Forest country park immediately north of the village. The tourist guide also describes other good things, such as the wonderful town of Newark, literary associations such as D H Lawrence and Lord Byron, and the City of Nottingham itself.

These are all major interests, but there is far more to Nottinghamshire than these. Along the western edge is limestone country on the far periphery of the Peak District, and to the south of Nottingham the county includes much of the rolling Vale of Belvoir, with its Blue Lias building stone. The sandstone belt runs in a wide swathe north from Nottingham Castle's bluff and out of the county into Yorkshire. It underlies the thin, unproductive soils of Sherwood Forest and is, in a way, the reason it exists: the land was no good for tillage, only for trees, heaths, hunting and rabbit warrens. The land improves further north, with better soils around Blyth.

East of the sandstone, the land is marly and productive. The landscape is typically Midland, with villages set in rolling gentle hills. The fields are mostly 18th-century enclosure ones, and there are several country houses in parks (though many more houses, including Ossington Hall, have been demolished). Laxton village is a very rare survival of the medieval open-field farming system that the 18th-century Enclosure Acts extinguished. Here, the village is surrounded by three great hedgeless fields, where crops are rotated and the fields are farmed in common. This remarkable survival of medieval practice is now carefully safeguarded and is a major feature of interest in the county.

Further east, the River Trent in its wide flat valley runs along the eastern boundary of Nottinghamshire, having entered the county near Nottingham to flow north-east to Newark. The Trent valley is notable for the clusters of huge cooling towers associated with power stations, which were originally supplied with coal from the Nottinghamshire coalfields by river barge, or from elsewhere via the Humber estuary and then the Trent.

To the far north the land again is very flat, part of it including the Carrs, former marshes with vast skies of towering clouds, which were drained by Dutchmen in the 17th century. Drainage was not popular with the local population, as it robbed those villages on the marsh edges of their wild fowling and reed beds.

Nottinghamshire is not a county of extremes: the highest points are close to the Derbyshire border, west of Mansfield, and are little over 550ft. Robin Hood Hill, west of Southwell, is 473 ft (the peak itself is actually called Loath Hill, but is part of Robin Hood Hill which is much more apposite). The lowest point in the county is about six feet above sea level, where the River Idle flows through Misterton Carr.

Sherwood Forest is described in the introduction to Chapter 5, but the best surviving areas are found in the Dukeries (a group of estates owned by four dukes, including the Dukes of Newcastle and Portland), although they have been given the 18th- and 19th-century landscape treatment. For example, the Clumber estate is entered via lodge gates and screens, some of which have great architectural presence, such as the Apleyhead Gate. There are also great lime avenues, parkland trees and cropped grass swards, lakes and many other beautifications, including temples, grottoes and alcoves. The other great dukery estates are similarly landscaped, but there are also large expanses of more natural landscape, containing oak, birch and bracken.

Further south, Sherwood Forest country park, situated north and north-west of Edwinstowe, is the most publicly accessible part of the forest, and is little changed in character since the Middle Ages. Although many of the trees are post-medieval, their pattern and appearance duplicates the medieval forest before its take-over by the Dukes and others. Here, stag-headed ancient oaks of wide girth are dotted among birch and young oak woodland with bracken ground cover. Many of the oldest trees are in a state of collapse, but one survives as a tourist attraction: the 800-year-old Major Oak. Its ancient boughs are propped, and its rootspread area is fenced off, but the mile-and-a-half circuit from the visitor centre is well trodden.

Within the forest are coal mines and former coal mines, and it is important to remember that the Dukes of Newcastle owed much of their wealth to the Black Gold. Coal-mining occupied the whole of the western areas of Nottinghamshire; there are numerous villages that owe their existence to King Coal, a life brought vividly to worldwide audiences by the county's most famous miner's son D H Lawrence, whose birthplace in Eastwood is now a museum.

The city of Nottingham is situated at the end of the sandstone belt, which finishes abruptly with the 130ft-high Castle Rock, and on the more gentle slopes immediately to its east. Nottingham is now very large, with a population of over 250,000, but it is also a very fine city with an historic core of great interest and quality. It was presumed to be originally settled by the charmlessly-named 'Snot' or 'Snota'. Place-names ending in '-ingham' are early Anglo-Saxon ones, and excavations have revealed evidence to back this up on the eastern of the two hills on which the city now stands. Snot's settlement later became a burh on the same hill - the word is still in use nowadays as 'borough'.

In 867 AD, the destiny of the town changed with the arrival of

NEWARK-ON-TRENT, TRENT BRIDGE 1900 / 45104

the Danish armies, and at the Treaty of Wedmore in 878 AD it was absorbed into the Danelaw as one of the Five Boroughs (the others were Stamford, Leicester, Lincoln and nearby Derby). Danish place-names are common in the county, and include those ending in '-by' and '-thorpe'. The Norman Conquest of 1066 brought the most radical change, however: the erection of a castle on Castle Rock after 1068. This was improved and rebuilt in stone to become, in the 12th century, a very important royal castle. The Normans also established a new town, the 'French Borough' between the castle and the old Anglo-Saxon burh, the 'English Borough'. The present large market square was the heart of the French Borough. The heart of the old English Borough is the area around St Mary's church, High Pavement and the Lace Market.

To the east, and also on the River Trent, is the town of Newark, the second town in the county; in terms of the survival of historic fabric, it is now perhaps the first. It is even older than Nottingham, for many Romano-British archeological finds indicate a settlement here on the Roman Fosse Way road. Certainly, it was an Anglo-Saxon settlement

MANSFIELD, CHURCH STREET 1949 / M184007

that after the Norman Conquest was used as the basis for the new town laid out by Alexander the Magnificent, Bishop of Lincoln. Again, it had a very large market place, set in the shadow of Alexander's great castle that guarded the Trent crossing (a crossing made on a timber bridge he had built). All this took place in the 1120s and 1130s.

The county was at the heart of the great events of the English Civil War. King Charles I raised his standard at Nottingham Castle in 1642, the first action of the War, although he soon left the town, which was strongly pro-Parliament. Newark, meanwhile, was staunchly Royalist, and was besieged three times, only surrendering in May 1646 when Charles himself ordered it from the Saracen's Head in Southwell as part of his attempted negotiations with the Scottish army encamped at Kelham. Newark is surrounded by fascinating Civil-War siegeworks, and there were numerous Royalist forays against Nottingham. The county provided 5 out of the 58 Regicides, that is, signatories of King Charles' death warrant in 1649. After the war, both Nottingham and Newark castles were 'slighted', or rendered useless. Fortunately for Newark, the river-front elevation survived the attention of a pressed labour force.

During the 18th century, the county assumed much of its present character, with near-universal use of clay pantiles for roofs, and brick everywhere for houses and cottages. Enclosure Acts divided up the open fields of the villages into neat hawthorn-hedged small fields, and industry arrived, particularly around Nottingham, which began to grow quickly. Cotton mills and machine-lace factories supplanted the home-workers' hand looms, stocking frames and lace bobbins. The mechanisation of industry and deep coal-mining transformed parts of the county, particularly the western half. In areas around Mansfield, for example, coal mines were thick on the ground, but they also pushed eastward to Edinstowe and beyond, with Harworth the most northerly. Much of the early industrial housing was poor, with Nottingham becoming notorious for its gross overcrowding in insanitary tiny cottages. Later in the 19th century, serried ranks of brick cottages were built to house miners and industrial workers.

Nottingham's industry diversified, thanks to local entrepreneurs such as Jesse Boot and John Player: the former developed a health empire, the latter did his best to counter it by manufacturing billions of cigarettes. Between the World Wars council housing sprang up, while the first middle-class houses were built in the early 19th century in The Park and areas north of the Arboretum, both in Nottingham.

After World War II, housing development continued, while in the town centres much was destroyed, apparently in the belief that to regenerate run-down areas, a total rebuild is needed. We can all think of prime examples of mistakes: none more so than the office blocks lining Nottingham's Maid Marian Way, or the extraordinary crassness of Market Square House. Maid Marian Way and various developments in the city, such as the Victoria Centre or the Broad Marsh Centre, can be echoed in other towns. Mansfield, for example, suffered an insensitive inner ring-road, coyly named St Peter's Way, and got its own shopping centre, the Four Seasons, to replace its older townscape. Fortunately, this phase has passed its peak; the visitor can appreciate the finer points of this wonderful county, for despite the Robin-Hoodery of the image-makers, Nottinghamshire remains stubbornly individualistic and resistant to marketing men.

This book is dependent, to some extent, on what is in the Francis Frith Archive: for example, there are no views of Gingley on the Hill, Rufford Abbey, Shireoaks Hall, Holme Pierpoint, Besthorpe, the extraordinary Bunny Hall, and even large parts of the city of Nottingham, such as St Mary's church and the Lace Market area. I hope this collection, which shows the county from about 1890 to the 1960s, will encourage many who do not know this county to visit it and not merely thunder through on the East Coast main line or on the M1. It is well worth a tour - and not merely because my grandfather's family came from north Nottinghamshire.

NOTTINGHAM
CARRINGTON STREET

1890 / 22819

NOTTINGHAM
MARKET SQUARE

1890 / 22807

The view wonderfully captures the essence of the late Victorian market square, with its tight rows of stalls, the remains of the Georgian colonnaded piazza and the self-confident, ornate and large-scale Victorian replacements (the Italianate one on the left in its turn was replaced by Debenhams in the 1920s).

15

1902 / 48326

JACKSONS
DRURY HILL

STATION ST

18

On the right is the old Exchange, built in 1726. Besides numerous shops within the building, there were over 60 butchers' stalls or 'shambles'. This friendly, unhygienic mix was replaced in 1927 by the present Council House, in an overpowering, municipal baroque style with a giant portico and towering dome.

NOTTINGHAM THE OLD COUNCIL HOUSE AND MARKET SQUARE

1902 / 48321

NOTTINGHAM
MARKET SQUARE LOOKING
TOWARDS ANGEL ROW

1906 / 56461

By 1906, few of the Georgian buildings remain, and larger-scale Victorian and Edwardian ones have appeared. H Samuel and Hepworths survive, but the four Georgian buildings next to them have gone. The left of the view is now ruined by a particularly crass 1967 tower block, Market Square House.

Unveiled amid great pomp in 1905, the year before this view was taken, Albert Toft's then gleamingly fresh marble statue was moved to the Memorial Gardens on Victoria Embankment in 1953, making way for road widening. Its place has now been taken by a modern and anaemic bronze family of four.

NOTTINGHAM
QUEEN VICTORIA STATUE

1906 / 56462

To the left of Market Street corner is The Talbot, rebuilt in 1876 and now the celebrated Yates's Wine Lodge. The building on the opposite corner was soon to succumb to Debenhams, whose first two bays (in white stone) have already replaced two Victorian buildings.

NOTTINGHAM MARKET SQUARE LOOKING NORTH-EAST
1923 / 74594

NOTTINGHAM
LONG ROW, MARKET SQUARE

1890 / 22815

Further east along Long Row, all the buildings in this view have now been rebuilt, not necessarily for the better. A notable loss is the Georgian sashed-and-corniced, 16th-century white rendered building with dormer windows. Note the horse tram with the old Exchange beyond, another casualty from this view.

STATIONS
MARKET PLACE
SHERWOOD

PYATTS
THE FANCY DRAPER

PLAYERS NAVY

SHERWOOD

5

The flamboyant hotel in the middle distance was built in 1887 by the somewhat quirky Nottingham architect Watson Fothergill. Its lease expired in 1969, and its weirdly over-the-top architecture was swept away, to be replaced by the utterly gutless Littlewoods store. By 1902 the trams were electric-powered.

NOTTINGHAM
THE BLACK BOY
HOTEL
LONG ROW

1902 / 48326

The Georgian and mid 19th-century buildings on the left have their open colonnades fronting the market square intact. It is regrettable that only the very distant buildings, well beyond the Clumber Street junction, survive today. Those on the right, Smithy Row, were replaced by the grand stonework of the 1920s Council House complex.

NOTTINGHAM
LONG ROW

1890 / 22814

The plate-glass windows on the right belonged to one of the earliest Boot's chemist shops. Jesse Boot, one of Nottingham's most famous sons and a great benefactor to the city, started life in his widowed mother's herbalist shop, and went on to found the Boot's Pure Drug Company in 1888.

NOTTINGHAM
PELHAM STREET

1890 / 22823

Beyond the last building in Poultry, with its colonnade over the pavement, is Victoria Street, with its grand Victorian palazzos of commerce. The corner building survives, although without the oriel, as do most of the buildings further up Victoria Street, which are still used as commercial offices.

NOTTINGHAM VICTORIA STREET

1890 / 22817

Vast changes have occurred here since 1927. The Theatre Royal's fine stuccoed portico of 1865 survives, but the auditorium was wrapped in new extensions in the 1970s and the Royal Concert Hall was added behind, all in a successful modern style. The 1908 domed Hippodrome has gone, but the 1909 Westminster Building on the left survives.

NOTTINGHAM THEATRE SQUARE

1927 / 80550

NOTTINGHAM
CARRINGTON STREET LOOKING
NORTH FROM CANAL STREET

1890 / 22819

*This view looks from the canal towards Lister Gate. All
has gone, and the modern view is totally blocked by the
1960s Broad Marsh shopping centre. A 1920s block on
the left has copied the recessed curved corner, but on the
right corner is a multi-storey car park.*

NOTTINGHAM
WHEELER GATE

1902 / 48327

This view, taken from beside St Peter's churchyard, is now much changed on the left, although Eldon Chambers, the Georgian brick building with a semi-circular window, survives. More buildings remain on the right, however, including the former St Peter's hotel of the 1880s and the bay-windowed building beyond of 1886.

35

Originally the main crossing of the River Trent from the south, the present elegant cast-iron Trent Bridge dates from 1871 and was designed by the corporation engineer. Modern river cruisers continue to provide pleasure trips along the Trent, but no longer in the graceful steamers seen in this view.

NOTTINGHAM TRENT BRIDGE FROM THE NORTH-EAST

1902 / 48328

The view from the Victoria Embankment looks north to Trent Bridge, past rowing boats and other pleasure craft for hire moored at the steps. To the left of the bridge is the former Town Arms pub, now The Aviary. Beyond are factories and warehouses, replaced long ago by housing.

NOTTINGHAM
VICTORIA EMBANKMENT STEPS

1920 / 69443

The Sandstone bluff of Castle Rock can no longer be seen from Castle Wharf on the late 18th-century Nottingham Canal. This is because Castle Court of 1894 to the right, and Impact House of 1896 in the centre, now block the view entirely.

NOTTINGHAM CASTLE
FROM THE CANAL

1890 / 24699

NOTTINGHAM
THE CASTLE FROM THE
NORTH-WEST

1890 / 24698

The palace that the Duke of Newcastle built in the 1670s on the site of the castle's medieval upper bailey is seen here from the Park Estate. This well-planned estate was laid out in the castle's former park in the 1820s. The white brick houses in front of the castle date from 1856.

NOTTINGHAM
TRENT BRIDGE FROM
THE SOUTH BANK

1927 / 80552

This is a very famous pub with an evocative name. It consists of a 17th-century timber frame and 18th-century brickwork, and incorporates cellars cut into the sandstone of Castle Rock. Behind it is now the Brewhouse Yard Museum and the Angel Row Gallery, both utilising gabled brick houses of about 1680.

NOTTINGHAM
YE OLDE TRIP TO JERUSALEM
CASTLE ROCK

1920 / 69430

The bulk of the medieval castle, largely made a ruin by the Civil War, was 'slighted' or made useless by order of Parliament in 1651. Now only the outer bailey east walls and a 14th-century gatehouse survive, the latter showing its poor condition in 1902 prior to restoration.

NOTTINGHAM
THE OLD CASTLE GATEHOUSE

1902 / 48330

As we look across the outer bailey, now landscaped as a park, we can see the city centre beyond the back of the heavily-restored medieval gatehouse. Nowadays the view is interrupted by the rows of appalling 1960s office towers lining the Maid Marian Way ring road.

NOTTINGHAM
THE CASTLE GROUNDS

1920 / 69434

Jesse Boot gave money to landscape this area as public gardens, with
Wallis Gordon's great archway and colonnades as a focus. Beyond is
Victoria Embankment and the River Trent. The triumphal arch, with
its splendid green-painted wrought-iron gates, dates from 1927 and is
a notable landmark along the river.

NOTTINGHAM
THE ARCH OF REMEMBRANCE
VICTORIA EMBANKMENT

1928 / 81563

berk

From University Boulevard this view looks across the lake to the pristine new Portland limestone of Morley Horder's Trent Building. Started in 1922, its classical design set the university's building style until the 1960s. The university college was founded in 1877, but did not achieve fully-independent degree-conferring status until 1948.

NOTTINGHAM
THE TRENT BUILDING
NOTTINGHAM UNIVERSITY

1928 / 81574

NOTTINGHAM
WOLLATON HOUSE

1928 / 81579

The tide of Nottingham's expansion has swept round Wollaton House, one of the great Elizabethan houses. Designed by Robert Smithson for Sir Francis Willoughby, who made his fortune from coal, it was built in the 1580s and is set in 500 acres of park. The latter was bought by the corporation in 1925.

Seen from the A453, the main road into Nottingham on the north bank of the Trent, St Wilfrid's church, with its dignified battlemented 15th-century chancel, along with the old rectory and the Ferry Inn, make an attractive riverside grouping. Today Wilford has been absorbed into greater Bridgford.

WILFORD
ST WILFRID'S CHURCH

1890 / 24721

WEST BRIDGFORD
CENTRAL AVENUE

c1965 / W437005

From Church Drive and along Bridgford Road, it is a
short distance from the medieval heart of West Bridgford
to Central Avenue, a dull 1930s shopping parade
somewhat relieved by The Park. Most buildings survive,
but one block on the left has been rebuilt in replica.

The West Bridgford Hotel, spanking new (and hideous) in 1965, has found a new life as the Rushcliffe Civic Centre or council offices, but it does little for the setting of Trent Bridge. The floodlights beyond belong to Nottingham Forest football club, now with high grandstands around the pitch.

WEST BRIDGFORD
THE HOTEL AND TRENT BRIDGE

C1965 / W437008

Stapleford, now a satellite town of Nottingham, is renowned for its 11th-century Anglo-Saxon cross in St Helen's churchyard. Stapleford was a noted lace-making and framework-knitting village until it expanded in Victorian times. The chapel on the right has now been replaced by shops.

STAPLEFORD
DERBY ROAD

c1955 / S718035

This view of the river south of Newark gives an idea of its industrial base, with the Trent Brewery chimneys and, on the left, Parnham's Watermill seen beyond the dredger, keeping the water highway clear for commerce.

NEWARK-ON-TRENT
THE TRENT LOOKING NORTH

1906 / 56505

NEWARK-ON-TRENT
THE MARKET PLACE

1906 / 56491

Part of the north-west wall and the gatehouse remain, so from Trent Bridge the castle has the illusion of being complete. The larger windows and the oriel were added by Bishop Thomas Rotheram in the 1470s, softening the harsh military aspect of the castle.

NEWARK-ON-TRENT
THE CASTLE FROM TRENT BRIDGE

1923 / 74610

This view looks into the bailey of the castle. The Norman arch of the gatehouse, built in the 1130s by Alexander, Bishop of Lincoln, frames the south-west tower from which the curtain wall originally continued to Castle Gate. The walls then ran along Castle Gate, turning at Beast Market Hill to complete the circuit at the gatehouse.

NEWARK-ON-TRENT CASTLE GARDENS

1923 / 74614

The vaulted undercroft below the north-west tower dates from the time of Bishop Henry de Burghersh, who substantially reconstructed the castle in the 1320s. The undercroft was probably a storehouse, and had access to barges on the river via the watergate, which still survives.

NEWARK-ON-TRENT
THE CASTLE UNDERCROFT

1904 / 51735

The original curtain wall prevented this view into the bailey,
but it was later demolished by the victorious Parliament.
Besieged in 1642, 1644 and 1646, this Royalist stronghold
only surrendered when ordered to do so by King Charles I
from nearby Southwell in May 1646.

NEWARK-ON-TRENT
THE CASTLE AND THE GARDENS

1904 / 51732

NEWARK-ON-TRENT
TRENT BRIDGE, NORTH SIDE

1900 / 45104

Commissioned in 1775 by the Duke of Newcastle, the bridge was widened by footways and railings to each side in 1848. Beyond the steam tug is the old town wharf, now greatly improved with terraces and steps to form part of an attractive riverside walk (and car park).

63

The first recorded bridge over the River Trent was the timber one at the same crossing point built in the 12th century by Alexander, Bishop of Lincoln, who also built the castle. Apparently it lasted over 500 years until replaced by the present one in 1775.

NEWARK-ON-TRENT
TRENT BRIDGE, SOUTH SIDE

1890 / 24649

NEWARK-ON-TRENT
FROM TRENT BRIDGE

1909 / 61796

The superb tower and spire of St Mary's church looms beyond the fine Georgian houses of Castle Gate and Bar Gate. On the left is the extraordinary Ossington Coffee Palace towering above the river, intended to beckon to the tough wharfingers and boatmen with beguiling smells of coffee.

An alien intruder designed by the fashionable London architects Ernest George and Peto, the Ossington Coffee Palace opened in 1882 as a temperance hotel, covenanted for a century not to sell intoxicating liquors. The well-meaning Viscountess Ossington would no doubt be horrified to know that it is now a pub called The Ossington.

NEWARK-ON-TRENT OSSINGTON COFFEE PALACE, BEAST MARKET HILL

1890 / 24659

Nestling in the right corner is Ye Old White Hart, a superb 15th-century, timber-framed inn with its timbers brightly painted and restored to their original colours, which seem garish to modern eyes. To the left, at the top of Bridge Street, is G H Porter, a fine five-bay early Georgian building.

NEWARK-ON-TRENT
THE MARKET PLACE
LOOKING EAST

1890 / 24655

NEWARK-ON-TRENT
THE MARKET PLACE, NORTH SIDE

1900 / 45105

NEWARK-ON-TRENT
BRIDGE STREET LOOKING EAST

1906 / 56492

This is now a pedestrianised street; this view looks into the marketplace. On the corner to the right is a tall early Georgian house with a deep cornice and dormer windows, where Lord Byron's first volumes of poetry were published: these were 'Fugitive Pieces' in November 1806 and 'Hours of Idleness' in July 1807.

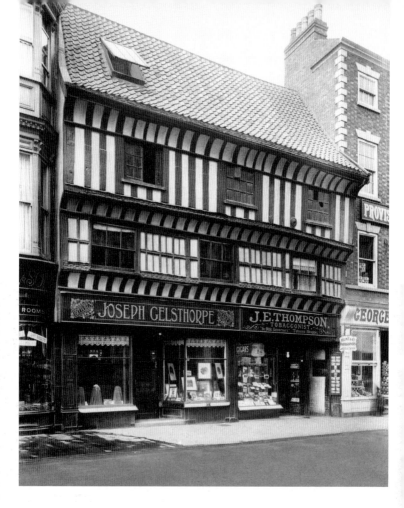

NEWARK-ON-TRENT
THE GOVERNOR'S HOUSE,
STODMAN STREET

1909 / 61804

*This view was taken from near Bridge
Street. The big tree in St Mary's churchyard
has gone, and the wall has been rebuilt
further back from the pavement. The
Newark Museum is in one of the distant
houses on the right and is well worth
visiting.*

NEWARK-ON-TRENT
APPLETON GATE LOOKING
NORTH-EAST

1906 / 56498

NEWARK-ON-TRENT
APPLETON GATE LOOKING
SOUTH-WEST

1909 / 61797

The Georgian houses on the right remain, and the tree beyond marks
St Mary's churchyard. On the left, however, the battlemented wall has
been replaced by the Palace Theatre, a bizarre 1920s oriental confection
complete with minarets - a sort of poor man's Taj Mahal.

The Wesleyan church on the right dates from 1844, and is typical of the big town chapels at that time. Next to it is the church hall, and beyond that the Rutland Arms: uneasy neighbours, no doubt, for temperate Wesleyans (nowadays known as Methodists).

NEWARK-ON-TRENT BARNBY GATE AND THE WESLEYAN CHURCH

1904 / 51742

NEWARK-ON-TRENT
KIRK GATE LOOKING TO
ST MARY'S CHURCH

1900 / 45106

NEWARK-ON-TRENT
THE POST OFFICE, KIRK GATE

1908 / 59944

This 15th-century cross was 'repaired and ornamented' in 1778, as recorded on an attached plaque. To see it now you have to go south-east to the London Road Gardens, where it was moved in 1974 because of road improvements at this busy junction.

NEWARK-ON-TRENT
BEAUMOND CROSS
CARTER GATE

1904 / 51740

Pleasure boating was very popular in late Victorian and Edwardian times, and the Trent at the weekends was alive with boats of all types. Admittedly, things look pretty quiet in this view of the river.

NEWARK-ON-TRENT
THE BOAT HOUSE

1909 / 61801

The River Devon was also popular for pleasure boats, as in this Edwardian view taken to the south of the Devon Bridge, which carried the old Fosse Way into Newark. Unfortunately, the delightful brick bridge has been replaced by a modern concrete one.

NEWARK-ON-TRENT
THE OLD DEVON BRIDGE
FARNDON ROAD

1909 / 61802

The minster's clergy houses are spaciously set in gardens along Church Street and Westgate, and mostly have 18th- or 19th-century façades. The core of the old town is along King Street and West Gate, seen in the distance here. The Admiral Rodney's 19th-century render conceals a Georgian façade.

SOUTHWELL
KING STREET LOOKING
TOWARDS WESTGATE

1920 / 69472

This small, delightful historic town is dominated by its superb minster church. Founded by the Archbishop of York before AD956 as a minster church for the area with its own body or college of priests (prebendaries), the archbishops had a palace here until the mid 17th century.

SOUTHWELL
THE MINSTER AND
WEST GATE

1924 / 75665

Seen here are the Norman crossing tower, 105 ft high, the north transept and the north porch. To the left is the Chapter House of 1288, with its pointed roof. Built for Archbishop John de la Romaine, it is justly famed for the superb foliage carving on its capitals and arches.

SOUTHWELL
THE MINSTER, THE CROSSING
TOWER AND NORTH TRANSEPT

1890 / 24095

The low two-storeyed rendered building on the left in the middle distance is the 16th-century, timber-framed Saracen's Head. Here, in May 1646, Charles I spent his last night of freedom. Tactfully, the pub changed its name from the King's Head to the Saracen's Head soon after Charles was beheaded.

SOUTHWELL
WESTGATE LOOKING
NORTH-EAST

1920 / 69469

The old town core survives more or less intact, circumscribed by the St Peter's Way inner ring-road. The market place is still a fine space, with its centrepiece the Gothic Bentinck Memorial of 1849 (funds for the project ran out so there is no statue), and the 1752 Moot Hall beyond.

MANSFIELD
THE MARKET
PLACE

c1955 / M184027

The left-hand side of West Gate mainly survives, while on the right, nothing remains until the gable with the five chimney pots. Everything has been replaced by the vast Four Seasons Shopping Centre built in the 1970s.

MANSFIELD
WEST GATE LOOKING
SOUTH-EAST

1949 / M184016

*Marks & Spencer's and Woolworth's, with their stone
fronts, are still the same, although the street has now been
pedestrianised. However, in 1949 traffic was sufficiently
infrequent to allow mother and child to amble safely down
the middle of the road.*

MANSFIELD
WEST GATE LOOKING
NORTH-WEST FROM THE
MARKET PLACE

1949 / M184011

MANSFIELD
CHURCH STREET

1949 / M184007

This view is taken from underneath the 1875 viaduct, which carries the railway over the centre of the town. This end of Church Street is little changed. The stone-fronted, late 18th-century houses on the left remain, contrasting with the grander post office on the right. Beyond is the Norman west tower of the parish church.

Nothing remains of this view looking up Stockwell Gate towards the Market Place. To the left is now the Four Seasons Centre, and to the right the Co-op department store. In the far, far distance are survivors of old Mansfield.

MANSFIELD
STOCKWELL GATE

1949 / M184010

The view along the High Street is taken from the town's market place: not one of Nottingham's most inspiring, but behind the photographer is the medieval parish church. Lord Byron was buried here in the family vault, after his body had been brought back from Greece in 1824.

HUCKNALL
HIGH STREET

c1965 / H373017

WORKSOP
THE PRIORY CHURCH
WEST FRONT

c1955 / W278053

This view looks uphill past the mock timber-framed façade of the Unicorn Hotel towards the market place. Bridge Street is now pedestrianised, with stylish benches for the weary. It is a good street with few jarring notes, and many late 18th- and early 19th-century façades stepping and curving sedately uphill.

WORKSOP
BRIDGE STREET
LOOKING SOUTH

C1955 / W278023

Retford was granted its charter in 1246 and its market place dates from soon after, although the town really prospered when the Great North Road was diverted through it in 1766. Unfortunately, Cask and Co and the grand pedimented building to the right have now gone.

RETFORD
MARKET SQUARE AND
THE TOWN HALL

1944 / R261001

We are looking from the town hall past the war memorial.
The Yorkshire Bank is a Georgian house with odd
architrave frames to the windows. The market place, now
mainly pedestrianised, funnels into Chapelgate; beyond is
St Swithun's parish church tower.

RETFORD
THE MARKET PLACE

c1955 / R261030

CLUMBER PARK HOUSE
FROM THE SOUTH-EAST

c1873 / 6628

The house was demolished in 1938, leaving the stables and offices only. It had a splendid setting by the lake, which was dug in the 1770s, but was no great shakes architecturally, consisting of a basic 1760s brick house cased in stone and enlarged and extended from 1814 to 1880, gradually assuming an Italianate style.

The medieval royal forest of Sherwood once covered over 100,000 Nottinghamshire acres. The Sherwood Forest county park has 450 of the best surviving acres; ancient gnarled oaks rear up amid silver birch, younger oak and bracken. None is larger than the famous eight-hundred-year-old Major Oak, now fenced off and its weary boughs propped.

EDWINSTOWE
THE MAJOR OAK
SHERWOOD FOREST

c1965 / E142035

CLUMBER PARK HOUSE
AND THE CHURCH

C1873 / 6632

'The Dukeries' was a name applied from the 18th century onwards to four post-Reformation ducal estates carved out of Sherwood Forest: Clumber, Thoresby, Welbeck and Worksop. Clumber was given to the Duke of Newcastle in 1707. In this view, the mansion and church are seen from across the lake: only the latter survives.

Most of the cloister buildings of this priory remain. The priory was founded around 1170 and incorporated into the post-Dissolution mansion, granted by Henry VIII to Lord Byron's ancestor, Sir John Byron, in 1539. The medieval glory, though, is the superbly-proportioned west front of the demolished priory church.

NEWSTEAD ABBEY FROM THE WEST

1890 / 22856

The cloister ranges surround the cloister garth, and this view of the east range has the priory's chapter-house arches on the ground floor. The house was added to and repaired after Lord Byron, the poet, sold the abbey in 1817, but it will always be associated with his ownership.

NEWSTEAD ABBEY
EAST SIDE

c1955 / N29018

KELHAM HALL
FROM ACROSS THE RIVER TRENT

1890 / 24696

The present Kelham Hall replaced a Georgian mansion burned down in 1857. George Gilbert Scott, the architect of St Pancras Station, used the then fashionable Gothic revival style, building in harsh red Retford brick and Ancaster limestone. A further oddity is the Byzantine chapel of 1927.

This is an archive view, for Ossington Hall, a Georgian mansion, was demolished in 1963, one of many country houses lost to Nottinghamshire. John Carr of York's 1782 parish church survives, as do the landscaped grounds, the lake and the terrace wall seen in this view: all of these are most romantic and picturesque.

OSSINGTON HALL

1913 / 66094

The priory, founded after 1120, had two west towers: one, of about 1230, remains, with elements of the nave incorporated within a Victorianised church. Today, the church reads as an appendage to the mainly 1777 house, Thurgarton Priory, now shorn of its ivy cloak. From the churchyard, though, the house is completely invisible.

THURGARTON PRIORY AND THE CHURCH

1890 / 24681

In this view looking north past the High Street junction, the bridge over the stream is marked with flood levels from 1795 to 1977. Beyond, the houses remain, albeit with modern windows, and the importance of the fine parish church to the street scene is evident here.

SUTTON-ON-TRENT CHURCH STREET

1913 / 66085

This tranquil scene shows the Gothic-style brick Methodist or Wesleyan church of 1878, beyond creeper-clad number 37 in the foreground. The road now has pavements on each side and modern infill houses at various points.

SUTTON-ON-TRENT
THE WESLEYAN CHURCH
AND HIGH STREET

1909 / 61817

From the other end of the High Street more change is evident now. The Edwardian houses on the left survive, but the long house with pantile roof beyond has been replaced by new houses in Forge Close. The one on the right has also gone.

SUTTON-ON-TRENT
THE HIGH STREET

1913 / 66087

Joseph Pocklington, who built Carlton Hall, was something of an amateur architect; he designed many of the buildings in the village. Much has changed since 1909: the building on the left now has a shallow modern roof, and the fine horse-chestnut tree has been replaced by new house.

CARLTON-ON-TRENT
THE VILLAGE

1909 / 61827

FARNDON
THE FERRY ACROSS
THE RIVER TRENT

1923 / 74627

Farndon has a mix of modern housing estates and a delightful old village around the church. North-east of the church, a lane leads to the former ferry across the River Trent, seen here heading for the Rolleston bank. In the background, the Britannia pub remains, but the swings have gone.

WINTHORPE
ALL SAINTS' CHURCH

1890 / 24688

*Beyond the Brownlow Arms at the east
end of the small village of Marnham, a
track leads to the River Trent bank. Here
a rowing-boat ferry once linked Marnham
with South Clifton on the Lincolnshire
bank, where most of the trees seen in this
view have since been felled.*

MARNHAM
THE FERRY

1913 / 66096

The village is south-east of Newark, but still within the A1 bypass.
All on the left beyond the Rose and Crown has been lost. To the right,
the late 14th-century crocketted spire of St Giles' church can be seen, a
church which is noted for its superb Norman south doorway.

BALDERTON
MAIN STREET LOOKING EAST

1909 / 61814

The chapel on the corner and the concrete telephone box
have gone, but the 1872 Board Schools remain. My great-
grandfather, Johnson Durdey, had a printing business in
Misterton and published annually Durdey's Almanack,
rather like Whitakers' but more local: it flourished from
1878 until after World War I.

MISTERTON
SCHOOL CORNER

c1955 / M235037

This view is taken from the Soss Lane bridge over the 1770s Chesterfield canal, with, to the left, the last lock before the Trent basin and, to the right, the canal-side Packet Inn, both out of view. The A161 bypasses this bridge, so Soss Lane is not a quiet backwater.

MISTERTON
THE ROAD TO THE RIVER TRENT

c1955 / M235002

Seen from the tall 15th-century west tower, so cavalierly inserted into the nave of the Norman Priory church, are some of the coaching inns from the Great North Road glory days, and houses in the estate style of red brick with Gothic patterned windows. Blyth Hall itself was demolished in 1972.

BLYTH
FROM THE PRIORY
CHURCH TOWER

c1955 / B605018

INDEX

PLEASE HELP US BRING FRITH'S PHOTOGRAPHS TO LIFE

Our authors do their best to recount the history of the places they write about. They give insights into how particular towns and villages developed, they describe the architecture of streets and buildings, and they discuss the lives of famous people who lived there. But however knowledgeable our authors are, the story they tell is necessarily incomplete.

Frith's photographs are so much more than plain historical documents. They are living proofs of the flow of human life down the generations. They show real people at real moments in history; and each of those people is the son or daughter of someone, the brother or sister, aunt or uncle, grandfather or grandmother of someone else. All of them lived, worked and played in the streets depicted in Frith's photographs.

We would be grateful if you would tell us about the many places shown in our photographs—the streets with their buildings, shops, businesses and industries. Describe your own memories of life in those streets: what it was like growing up there, who ran the local shop and what shopping was like years ago; if your workplace is shown tell us about your working day and what the building is used for now. With your help more and more Frith photographs can be brought to life, and vital memories preserved for posterity.

We will gradually add your comments and stories to the archive for the benefit of historians of the future. Wherever possible, we will try to include some of your comments in future editions of our books. Moreover, if you spot errors in dates, titles or other facts, please let us know, because our archive records are not always completely accurate—they rely on 150 years of human endeavour and hand-compiled records.

So please write, fax or email us with your stories and memories. Thank you!

FREE PRINT OF YOUR CHOICE

Choose any Frith photograph in this book.
Simply complete the Voucher opposite and
return it with your remittance for £2.25 (to
cover postage and handling) and we will print
the photograph of your choice in SEPIA (size
11 x 8 inches) and supply it in a cream mount
with a burgundy rule line
(overall size 14 x 11 inches).
**Please note: photographs with a reference number
starting with a "Z" are not Frith photographs and
cannot be supplied under this offer.**
Offer valid for delivery to UK one address only.

Mounted Print
Overall size 14 x 11 inches (355 x 280mm)

PLUS: **Order additional Mounted Prints at
HALF PRICE - £7.49 each** (normally £14.99)
If you would like to order more Frith prints
from this book, possibly as gifts for friends and
family, you can buy them at half price (with no
additional postage and handling costs).

PLUS: **Have your Mounted Prints framed**
For an extra £14.95 per print you can have your
mounted print(s) framed in an elegant polished
wood and gilt moulding, overall size
16 x 13 inches (no additional postage and
handling required).

IMPORTANT!

These special prices are only
available if you use this form to
order. You must use the ORIGINAL
VOUCHER (no copies permitted).

We can only despatch to one
UK address. This offer cannot be
combined with any other offer.

FRITH PRODUCTS AND SERVICES

All Frith photographs are available for you to buy as framed or mounted prints.
From time to time, other illustrated items such as Address Books and Maps are also
available. Already, almost 80,000 Frith archive photographs can be viewed and
purchased on the internet through the Frith website.

For more detailed information on Frith companies and products, visit:

www.francisfrith.co.uk

For further information, or trade enquiries, contact:

The Francis Frith Collection, Frith's Barn, Teffont, Salisbury SP3 5QP

Tel: +44 (0) 1722 716 376 Fax: +44 (0) 1722 716 881 Email: sales@francisfrith.co.uk